GRAE*ae*

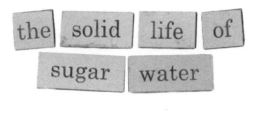

the solid life of sugar water

Jack Thorne

The Solid Life of Sugar Water was previewed at The Drum,
Theatre Royal Plymouth, from Monday 8th to Saturday 13th June 2015,
with a run at the Pleasance Dome, Edinburgh Festival Fringe,
from Wednesday 5th to Sunday 30th August 2015

A NOTE ON THE PLAY

Graeae casts Deaf and disabled people in plays that do
not specify whether a character is or is not Deaf or disabled.

Sugar Water is in its essence a play about a young couple in an
intense and moving relationship and the events that take place can
and have happened to any two people, disabled and non-disabled
alike. The decision to ask Jack to write some references to being Deaf
and disabled came from the fact that they accept and loved those
things about each other. It is part of the authenticity of their
communication; who they are as people and who they are with each
other. The play doesn't hide away from anything and we felt we
could gain so much by having a playfulness and freedom around
access which Jack has poignantly and humorously captured.

This is the glorious thing about Graeae and how we creatively use
these elements as part of a whole, getting the actors to a place where
people could believe their relationship; right from their access, their
pain and their fundamental love for each other. Our unique way of
working informs the rationale for creative captioning and audio
description for our audiences, which generates an excitement of
pushing the boundaries of what is theatrically possible.

Amit Sharma, Director

CAST

ALICE	**Genevieve Barr**
PHIL	**Arthur Hughes**

CREATIVE TEAM

Writer	**Jack Thorne**
Director	**Amit Sharma**
Designer	**Lily Arnold**
Producer	**Emma Dunstan**
Lighting Designer	**Ian Scott**
Sound Designer/Composer	**Lewis Gibson**
Movement Director	**Cathy Waller**
Voice Coach	**Chris Holt**
Casting Director	**Sarah Hughes**

PRODUCTION TEAM

Production Manager	**Hugh Borthwick**
Company Stage Manager	**Rosie Giarratana**
Technical Stage Manager	**Drew Baumohl**
Costume Supervisor	**Lorna Price**
Wardrobe Mistress	**Cheryl Hill**
Drum Technician	**Matt Hoyle**
Head of Sound	**Dan Mitcham**
LX Practicals	**Chris Blackler**
Set, costumes and props by	**Theatre Royal Plymouth**
Audio Description	**Wayne 'Pickles' Norman**
Production photography	**Patrick Baldwin**
Production filming	**Ted Evans for Defeye Films**
Marketing artwork	**Dragonfly Design**

With thanks to: **Essential Supplies, Hackworthy & Sons, ADS Window Films Ltd.**

BIOGRAPHIES

ALICE | **GENEVIEVE BARR**

Genevieve's acting career started with the lead role of Amelia in BBC drama series *The Silence*. She was subsequently nominated for a BAFTA for Best Actress for this role. Television credits include *Shameless*, BAFTA award-winning drama series *The Fades*, *The Amazing Dermot*, *True Love* and *Call the Midwife*.

Genevieve's theatre debut was in 2013 touring the UK with *Translations* by Brian Friel (Millennium Forum) and directed by Adrian Dunbar.

PHIL | **ARTHUR HUGHES**

Arthur trained at the Royal Welsh College of Music & Drama, graduating in 2013. He joined the BBC Radio Drama Company after becoming a recipient of the Carleton Hobbs Bursary Award.

Theatre credits include: *Bedazzled: A Welshman in Scotland* (Welsh tour/St. Andrews Byre Theatre); *TRACY* (White Bear, Kennington).

TV includes: *Doctors* (BBC Birmingham). Radio credits include: for BBC Radio 4: *Sword of Honour*, *Listening to the Dead*, *The Oresteia*, *Pilgrim*, *Home Front*, *Ordeal by Innocence*, *The Other Simenon*, *For Whom the Bell Tolls*, *The Real Trial of Oscar Wilde*, *Democracy for Beginners*.

WRITER | **JACK THORNE**

Theatre includes: *Hope* (Royal Court); *Let the Right One In* (Dundee Rep/ Royal Court, NTS/Marla Rubin Ltd.); *The Borough* (Punchdrunk/Aldeburgh Festival); *Stuart: A Life Backwards* (adapt. Hightide/Sheffield Theatre – Edinburgh Festival/tour); *Mydidae* (Drywrite – Soho/Trafalgar Studios); *The Physicists* (adapt. Donmar Warehouse); *Bunny* (Nabokov – UK tour/ NYC); *Red Car Blue Car, Two Cigarettes, When You Cure Me* (Bush); *Greenland* (National Theatre); *2nd May 1997* (Bush/Nabokov), *Burying Your Brother in the Pavement* (NT Connections) *and Stacy* (Tron/Arcola/ Trafalgar Studios).

Television: *Don't Take My Baby*, *Glue*, *The Fades* (Best Drama Series – BAFTA 2012), *This Is England '88* (Best Mini-Series – BAFTA 2012) and *This is England '86*, *Cast-Offs* and episodes of *Skins* and *Shameless*.

Film: *War Book*, *A Long Way Down* and *The Scouting Book for Boys* (Best British Newcomer – London Film Festival 2010).

DIRECTOR | **AMIT SHARMA**

Amit Sharma has been Graeae's Associate Director since 2011, and is a graduate from Graeae's Missing Piece actor training course. In summer 2012, Amit co-directed the outdoor spectacle *Prometheus Awakes* (with La Fura dels Baus/co-commissioned by GDIF and SIRF), marking the first large-scale outdoor production to be artistically led by Deaf and disabled people in the UK. Also for Graeae, he directed Ted Hughes' *The Iron Man* which toured both nationally and internationally and co-directed Graeae's Rhinestone Rollers in *Sequins and Snowballs* with Jenny Sealey at the Southbank Centre. As Assistant Director, he has worked on Graeae's productions of *The Threepenny Opera, The Changeling* and on *The Four Fridas* for Greenwich and Docklands International Festival 2015. He has worked extensively as an actor and director for various companies including the BBC, the National Theatre, Tamasha Theatre Company, East 15 Drama School and the Unicorn where he was part of the Ensemble. Amit currently leads on Write to Play, Graeae's flagship new-writing programme in partnership with venues across the UK.

DESIGNER | **LILY ARNOLD**

Training: Wimbledon College of Art. Theatre and opera: *The Jew of Malta, King Lear, The Taming of The Shrew, The Rape of Lucrece* (RSC); *Beached* (Marlowe Studios/Soho); *The Edge of our Bodies, Gruesome Playground Injuries* (Gate); *Peddling* (HighTide); *Minotaur* (Polka); *World Enough and Time* (Park); *The Boss of It All* (Assembly Roxy/Soho); *A Season in the Congo* and *The Scottsboro Boys* (Young Vic, Clare Space); *Happy New* (Trafalgar Studios); *Ahasverus* (Hampstead Downstairs); *A Midsummer Night's Dream* (Cambridge Arts Theatre); *Opera Scenes* (National Opera Studio); *Red Handed* (The Place, London). Website: lilyarnold.co.uk

LIGHTING DESIGNER | **IAN SCOTT**

Ian trained at Mountview. Recent work includes: *Sex and the Three Day Week* (Liverpool Playhouse); *Curlew River* (Barbican/Lincoln Center/UCLA Berkeley); *My Name is…* (Tamasha) and *Owen Wingrave* (Aldeburgh/ Edinburgh International Festival). Ian has worked with Graeae on many productions including: *Peeling, Blasted, Static* (with Suspect Culture), *Reasons to be Cheerful* and most recently *Blood Wedding* (with Dundee Rep & Derby Theatre). Other theatre credits include: *Frozen* (Fingersmiths & Birmingham Rep) and *Where the Wild Things Are / Higglety Pigglety Pop!* (Aldeburgh Music & LA Philharmonic).

SOUND DESIGNER/COMPOSER | **LEWIS GIBSON**

Lewis studied music at Dartington College of Arts. He is an associate artist with Uninvited Guests (*It Is Like It Ought To Be, Make Better Please, The Good Neighbour*), a founding member of the Arab/Anglo company SABAB (*In the Eruptive Mode, The Speaker's Progress, Richard III – An Arab Tragedy, The Mirror for Princes, Al-Hamlet Summit*) and long-term collaborator with Graeae (*The Iron Man, Belonging, The Limbless Knight, The Garden*).

As a writer, director and composer he has made a number of pieces of young people's theatre with the Royal Exchange, Tangere Arts and the Unicorn including *Tin Soldier* (winner OFFIE Best Young People's Show 2012), *A Thousand Slimy Things, The Pardoner's Tale* and *The Chair*. He has received commissions for sound art works from the V&A, Tate Britain, Shunt Lounge, Museum of London and Historic Royal Palaces.

MOVEMENT DIRECTOR | **CATHY WALLER**

Winner of the London Dance Award in 2012, Cathy Waller has worked nationally and internationally as a Choreographer and Movement Director for a variety of dance and theatre companies. Working as resident choreographer of Dance Offensive 2007–2012, Cathy has since created work for the BBC, Breakin' Convention and Tate Modern amongst others. After being awarded the Blueprint Bursary, commissioned by East London Dance and Sadler's Wells, Cathy created Cathy Waller Company, working with dancers and live musicians to create a new artistic vision, focusing on the interaction between rhythm, sound and vigorously challenging contemporary movement. The Company completed a seventeen-date tour in 2012, including performances at Sadler's Wells Sampled, West End Live and the National Theatre. Since their first successful tour, the company have gone on to create outdoor work, commissioned by Without Walls, Brighton Festival and Gi20, and will be performing a brand new indoor Double Bill Tour in 2016.

VOICE COACH | **CHRISTOPHER HOLT**

Christopher Holt has worked as an actor, singer, theatre director and theatre lecturer for twenty-five years. He gained his first degree from Middlesex Polytechnic in Performing Arts and then a second in Theatre Directing at the Royal Holloway University, University of London. His stage work has included *The Lion King*, *Les Misérables* and *Cats*. He has appeared at venues as large as Wembley Stadium and as intimate as the Donmar Warehouse. He has worked as voice coach on several Graeae plays over the last decade including *Bent*, *Whiter than Snow*, *Reasons to be Cheerful* and *The Threepenny Opera*. He has recently been working with Outside Edge as assistant director and dramaturg on their new production.

GRAE*ae*

THEATRE COMPANY

Graeae is a force for change in world-class theatre – breaking down barriers, challenging preconceptions and boldly placing Deaf and disabled artists centre stage.

Artistically led by Jenny Sealey MBE, Graeae's signature characteristic is the compelling creative integration of sign language, audio description and captioning, which engages brilliantly with both disabled and non-disabled audiences. Championing accessibility and providing a platform for new generations of artists, Graeae leads the way in pioneering, trail-blazing theatre.

Recent productions include: *Blood Wedding* (in co-production with Dundee Rep Ensemble and Derby Theatre), *The Threepenny Opera* (in co-production with West Yorkshire Playhouse, New Wolsey Theatre Ipswich, Nottingham Playhouse Company and Birmingham Repertory Theatre), *Belonging* (in co-production with Circo Crescer e Viver) and *Reasons to be Cheerful*. Spectacular outdoor productions in recent years have included *The Limbless Knight – A Tale of Rights Reignited* (in association with Strange Fruit/ commissioned by GDIF), *Prometheus Awakes* (with La Fura dels Baus/ co-commissioned by GDIF and SIRF) and *The Iron Man*.

Through its broad training programme, Graeae develops the next generation of Deaf and disabled artists through groundbreaking programmes and courses including: *Write to Play*, a bold new-writing initiative committed to developing the skills and experience of new writers in collaboration with some of the most creative minds in the industry. Throughout the year, Graeae runs a continuing professional development programme as well as workshops and training programmes internationally from Brazil to Bangladesh.

Graeae also widens participation and works extensively with young people through its outreach programme. Workshops and residencies run by our pool of Deaf and disabled facilitators in a variety of formal and informal education settings help to build new audiences, engage young creative minds and empower young disabled artists.

Artistic Director/CEO
Jenny Sealey MBE

Supported using public funding by
ARTS COUNCIL ENGLAND
LOTTERY FUNDED

THEATRE ROYAL PLYMOUTH

The Theatre Royal Plymouth is the largest and best attended regional producing theatre in the UK and the leading promoter of theatre in the South West. We produce and present a broad range of theatre in our three distinctive performance spaces - The Lyric, The Drum and The Lab - including classic and contemporary drama, musicals, opera, ballet and dance.

We specialise in the production of new plays and have built a national reputation for the quality and innovation of our programme. Our extensive creative learning work is pioneering and engages young people and communities in Plymouth and beyond. Our award winning waterfront production and learning centre, TR2, is a unique building with unrivalled set, costume, prop-making and rehearsal facilities.

Recent Theatre Royal Plymouth productions include *After Electra* by April de Angelis, *Grand Guignol* and *Horse Piss for Blood* by Carl Grose, *Merit* by Alexandra Wood, *Another Place* by DC Moore, *Chekhov in Hell* by Dan Rebellato, *The Astronaut's Chair* by Rona Munro, *Solid Air* by Doug Lucie and *Mad Man* by Chris Goode.

The Theatre Royal Plymouth also collaborates with some of the best artists and theatre makers in the UK and beyond. We have regularly co-produced with Paines Plough (*The Angry Brigade* by James Graham, *Love Love Love* by Mike Bartlett), Ontroerend Goed (*Fight Night, Sirens, All That is Wrong*), Frantic Assembly (*Othello, The Believers* by Bryony Lavery, *Lovesong* by Abi Morgan) and Told by and Idiot (*My Perfect Mind, And the Horse You Rode In On*).

Chief Executive: **Adrian Vinken OBE**
Artistic Director: **Simon Stokes**
Executive Producer: **Victoria Allen**
Marketing and Communications Director: **Marianne Locatori**
Operations Director: **Helen Costello**

Board of Directors
Chairman: **Sir Michael Lickiss**
Vice Chair: **Mrs Janie Grace**

Board Members
Mr Nick Buckland OBE, Mr Francis Drake, Ms Bronwen Lacey, Mr Robin Tatam, Mr Peter Vosper, Mr Paul Woods.

Supported using public funding by
ARTS COUNCIL ENGLAND

THE SOLID LIFE OF SUGAR WATER

Jack Thorne

For Chloe Sophia Moss

Sands
Stillbirth & neonatal death charity

Sands, the stillbirth and neonatal death charity, was established by bereaved parents in 1978.

Sands supports anyone affected by the death of a baby; works in partnership with health professionals to improve the quality of care and services offered to bereaved families; and promotes and funds research and changes in practice that could help to reduce the loss of babies' lives. It is a national organisation, with around 100 regional support groups across the UK.

Thousands of babies tragically die each year. In 2013, 5712 babies were stillborn or died soon after birth in the UK, shattering the lives of expectant parents, their families and their friends and the people who have cared for them.

Stillbirth is not a rare event and it's a tragedy that doesn't discriminate. Although the UK's stillbirth rate has fallen slightly in recent years, it remains unacceptably high. More research is needed to help identify babies at risk and reduce the loss of babies' lives.

Sands would not exist without the generosity of its supporters. Every penny raised is gratefully received and helps to fund and expand its vital work.

To find out how to get involved or donate to this charity please **visit www.uk-sands.org**

The author's proceeds from sales of this book are being donated to this charity.

Characters

ALICE, *twenty-nine*
PHIL, *thirty-one*

ALICE. I push his hand down...

PHIL. She feels softer, lying back – she's sprawled –

ALICE. Down over my body...

PHIL. Over her breasts – which are – just lying there, not erect... or...

Not that that – she's not got the greatest nipples...

ALICE. Over my belly...

PHIL. She's still got the slightly gloopy baby-fat thing going...

It doesn't feel like real fat it feels more – gloopy... full of...

ALICE (*giggle*). He's shaking.

PHIL. Liquid.

Water.

Gel.

ALICE. His body has this sheen to it. He's shaking.

PHIL. She hasn't washed much recently...

ALICE. We haven't washed much recently.

PHIL. She hasn't washed much recently.

ALICE. You're shaking.

PHIL. I'm fine –

ALICE. You're shaking. It's nice.

PHIL. I'm fine.

I'm desperate. Apart from anything else –

ALICE. First time since –

PHIL. I avoid her vagina and indeed the whole pubic region as I descend, I swerve to the left slightly to –

ALICE. First time since –

PHIL. I put my fingers on her inner thigh.

Inner thigh.

Just by her inner thigh.

And I sort of trace her inner thigh with the edges of my fingernails… She's got stretch marks in a few places…

ALICE. He touches my creases – my pockmarks. Fat marks. Creases. Sad marks. Happy.

PHIL. I trace her – graze her – inner thigh with just the edge of my – edge of my fingers.

ALICE. He always fucks around a bit…

PHIL. And I sort of do this thing – this circular movement – circle – circular – where I'm gently massaging – with the edge of my fingers – getting higher and higher…

ALICE. It's not – I mean, he's no –

PHIL. Touching the beginnings of pubic hair.

She hasn't done her bikini line in months so… That's not as high as it should be. The pubic hair feels greasy.

ALICE. I want to grab his hand. I want to hurt his hand.

PHIL. And then I just gently nudge her clit with the side of my little finger.

ALICE *pulls a face. Takes an intake of breath.*

Her fleshy clit.

It's not particularly fleshy today but I just gently nudge.

ALICE *pulls another face. Again the sharp breath.*

Nudge.

Nurdle.

ALICE. I circle my hand around his…

PHIL. She takes my hand around hers.

   I hate it when she –

ALICE (*giggle*). And I push his hand in towards me –

   She takes a series of breaths. Is she enjoying this?

PHIL. She feels the need, the need for speed.

ALICE. I push his hand –

PHIL. She always tries to…

ALICE. I push his hand –

PHIL. I –

ALICE. He pulls his hand away from mine.

PHIL. I –

ALICE. He pulls his hand away – my hand – away from me –

   Pause.

PHIL. And – break – and that's darts, ladies and gentlemen.

   Pause.

ALICE. He pulls his hand away from mine.

   Not a hard pull – but a – pull… A – pull. He pulls his hand
   away from mine.

   Pause.

PHIL. As my dad once said to me, if I wanted to be guided, I'd
   have bought a map.

   I think that was my dad.

   And I like maps.

   Pause.

   I've got this technique with my fingers… for when I enter.

ALICE. His fingers approach faster now.

   He's probably sorry for the – pull.

PHIL. A technique taught from centuries…

A technique thought up by monks and dragons.

Or – maybe – just made up – invented – by me.

Invented sounds better than made up.

ALICE. His fingers approach fast. He is sorry for the – pull.

He starts to enter me…

ALICE *pulls a face. Again the mini-breath.*

PHIL. I mean, I say technique… no, it's a technique.

ALICE. He starts to – enter me.

More breaths.

PHIL. She's not much of a clitoral girl. It's all about the hole for her.

Which is, which was – well, who am I to judge?

ALICE. I always like it when I'm first entered.

More breaths.

PHIL. It's sort of the bend-and-stretch technique.

ALICE. He –

More breaths.

PHIL. Or I like to call it an – air technique.

I put two fingers in – and then I sort of splay them apart as far as I can.

Sort of splay them apart. It's magic.

ALICE. He – oh.

She stops getting excited.

PHIL. Let the air into her just to… I don't know what it does.

ALICE. That –

PHIL. Okay?

ALICE. Yeah, just…

PHIL. Okay?

ALICE. Yeah.

PHIL. I say magic. I say mine. It's probably not an original technique.

I'm sure other men do it. Not that I've discussed it with them. It beats blowing on it. You can blow on it yourself, but air does the trick just as well. With the fingers splayed. You can just use natural air. Not your own.

The 'air' technique.

ALICE. He –

PHIL. I really don't like going down on a girl. And I'm not going down on her. She hasn't washed for ever…

ALICE. He –

PHIL. And then I stop the air technique – air magic – trademarked – and start exploring with my fingers.

ALICE. Finally he –

More breaths.

PHIL. In. Out. Shake it all about.

Try and build a rhythm and explore, at the same time, you know?

More breaths.

ALICE. I like his fingers inside me.

I like –

I'm not –

I'm pretty ripped up. Tender in places I haven't –

More breaths.

PHIL. Still with the two fingers I used for the splaying.

Now exploring.

I've been able to start with two fingers inside her since our second wedding anniversary. Before that it was…

More breaths.

ALICE. His breath becomes very – regulated…

PHIL. Her pelvic floor is not what it was –

More breaths.

ALICE. Breathe in.

PHIL. In.

More breaths.

ALICE. Breathe out.

PHIL. Out.

More breaths.

ALICE. He's very studied. I like the fact he's studied. I mean, sometimes I hate it, but mostly I like the fact he's studied.

PHIL. She's not that wet yet.

She's got that sort of leftover moisture inside her.

ALICE. Breathe in.

More breaths. But they're starting to sound affected. Not real.

PHIL. When she was pregnant it was one finger again – she was so tight, and you could feel the weight of the baby on your – and that's – amazing –

ALICE. Breathe out

PHIL. – I know I'm not supposed to think…

ALICE. Two fingers going anywhere, going in different directions…

Two fingers. Exploring. In me. In me.

Two fingers inside me. Three fingers.

PHIL. Three fingers.

ALICE. Penetrating me.

More breaths. Very artificial now.

PHIL. Like –

ALICE. That.

PHIL. Like –

ALICE. That.

PHIL. And then I stop and let her do the work… She likes this bit.

ALICE. He just leaves his fingers inside me. As if he's had enough of trying, he always does this.

PHIL. I always do this. It's like – pretending your fingers are a dildo. But she's not allowed to use her hands to move them.

Them.

It.

My finger dildo. Just her hips and her vaginal – whatever they're called.

ALICE. I try and do these sort of pelvic movements.

PHIL. She loves this. She always has.

ALICE. And then I –

PHIL. She sort of – I mean, she doesn't need a map.

She gets a sort of trance-like squeaky rhythm building up.

Eh – Eh – Eh – Eh. I move my thumb around, so that it's pressing against her anus while she moves her hips against my fingers…

ALICE. And I feel like I've something on my chest. In my chest.

PHIL. Eh-Eh-Eh-Eh. Her anus is still the – I like the word anus.

ALICE. Just this feeling in my chest.

PHIL. E-e-E-e-E-e.

ALICE. This fucking –

PHIL. But then E-e– ah – ow…

ALICE. Fucking –

PHIL. Her pelvis bone – some bone – a bone – has been newly exposed or something and one of my fingers gets trapped in there – under, or – I don't know, but she's sort of bending it backwards – it's being moved away from itself – one finger is fine and she's moving hard at that one – E-e-E-e- but because she's banging away – the finger that's trapped – the top bit is being moved away from the joint, my finger – and it's like she's trying to snap it –

ALICE. Fucking –

PHIL. I try and twist it away – I try and release it without her noticing – surely she should have noticed – I suppose it depends on how reactive a vagina is – but it's really trapped – I'm in the really fleshy bit – she's still not wet.

She's still gunky and my finger's really starting to –

ALICE. Fucking –

PHIL. Ow – sorry –

Beat.

ALICE. What?

PHIL. My finger it's –

ALICE. What?

PHIL. I, uh…

ALICE. You –

PHIL. I, uh… my finger's trapped inside you're…

ALICE. Your finger's – what?

PHIL. Trapped? Trapped.

ALICE. There's not – trapped? Just take it out.

PHIL. I just… I can't.

ALICE. Right.

PHIL. I, uh…

ALICE. My – doesn't –

PHIL. Ow. It really… I know.

ALICE. Does it?

I take out his finger –

PHIL. I – careful…

ALICE. He's a bit dramatic about it.

PHIL. There. There. Ow.

ALICE. My (vagina) doesn't… I'm almost sure.

PHIL (*laugh*). It really hurts. Hurt. Sorry. Sorry.

ALICE. Right.

PHIL. Sorry.

ALICE. No, you said…

PHIL. Sorry.

ALICE. And then he just lies back, and I'm supposed to lie back with him.

Takes a break. Nursing his – finger.

PHIL. Sorry. Sorry.

It's fine. Now. The finger. If you're…

Sorry.

Beat.

ALICE. Yeah. Always hated the word 'sorry'.

Beat.

PHIL. We met at a post office in 2010.

It sounds apocryphal.

It wasn't.

ALICE. He was posting a huge package.

Which sounds like a metaphor for something else.

It isn't.

PHIL. Well, is meeting the future love of your life an apocryphal event?

I'm not sure the dictionary twists to that.

ALICE. This huge great big – box.

No metaphor.

PHIL. Actually I'm not entirely sure what apocryphal means.

ALICE. I was standing behind him.

I had a smaller package, his was clearly going to take ages to post, he didn't ask whether I wanted to go in front of him – so my first memory of him – mild annoyance…

PHIL. My little brother was travelling in Africa.

I thought it would be fun to send a care package, like the army get.

ALICE. And the post office had these queuing lanes.

Have these queuing lanes.

We were in these queuing lanes. Me behind him.

Him with the huge package. No metaphor. Me with the little one. No metaphor.

PHIL. Condoms and cake was what I thought I'd send.

Or things like condoms and cake, I wasn't sure cake would really travel.

And what started off small – grew to –

Sherbet Dip Dabs. Curry powder. Marmite. Fruit of the Loom T-shirts. Washing powder. Ecover naturally. Tea-tree facial cleanser.

Clearasil. Tomato soup. Baked Beans. Baked Beans. Lots of… Baked Beans. Parmesan cheese. Powdered. Real cheese wouldn't carry.

A dongle with some downloads. Won't tell you what, but nothing shocking. A rugby ball. A cricket ball. Some bouncy balls.

A man-sized box of Kleenex. Hurrah! Pirate ho!

I tend toward excitement.

A novelty ice-cube tray, some fridge magnets.

It was really heavy –

ALICE. And the package – his package – no metaphor – didn't quite fit down between the rails.

It was slightly too wide.

It couldn't quite rest over the rails either. It was too large to fit between the rails. And too small to rest on top.

He could have rested on one or other of the rails. Leaned it against himself. But for some reason he didn't think of that.

And he didn't – he really – didn't quite have the arm strength to carry it.

PHIL. I'm not a strong man.

ALICE. He's not a strong man. He has the shoulders of a much – what's the phrase he uses…

PHIL. I have the shoulders of a much younger woman.

ALICE. But I like that – I like that he's not…

PHIL. The shoulders of a much younger woman.

ALICE. Anyway, small shoulders, big package. Have I emphasised the lack-of-metaphor thing enough yet?

And each time the queue stopped – he had to basically force it down through the rails in order to put it on the floor.

He had to squeeze it down through the rails…

He should have leant it on one of the rails and then against himself. But I was enjoying watching him too much to advise him.

PHIL. It was a really big box.

I probably chose the box wrong too.

I thought since that I should have leaned it on one of the rails and then against myself.

But life's always easier in retrospect. And actually I wouldn't change what happened next for anything…

ALICE. The box – (*Laughs.*) and this really isn't metaphorical in the slightest – (*Laughs.*) the box – exploded.

PHIL. It burst, I think is the right –

And I'm not sure if you've ever seen cardboard explode, no, it didn't burst…

ALICE. It – exploded. (*Laughs.*) It went – everywhere.

PHIL. And I don't know whether you've ever seen people ducking – (*Laughs.*) and diving for cover in a post office.

But it really is quite a sight.

ALICE. It was like a jack-in-a-box.

It sprayed stuff from all sides. I don't know quite how – he must have packed really fucking weirdly. It just – combusted. The bottom and the top broke at the same time I think. It – combusted.

PHIL. Though it wasn't a landmine or a suicide bomb it was a rugby ball and an inflatable baa-baa fuck sheep.

ALICE. It went everywhere.

And he went everywhere with it.

PHIL. Don't ask. Another novelty present.

ALICE. And that's the thing about skinny guys. They're
naturally physically funny. You just want to laugh at them.

PHIL. I bought it online.

Like one of those dolls you fuck, but a sheep... Again, trying
to be... Na-nah.

ALICE. It wasn't that I wanted to help. I sort of had to. I got hit.

You can't avoid getting involved when you've been hit.

Everyone helped to be honest. After they'd stopped looking
scared.

After they'd looked at the skinny guy looking red-faced with
a broken box and realised he was totally entirely one-
hundred-and-forty-per-cent harmless.

PHIL. Frankly I'm just grateful no one understood what the
blow-up sheep was actually for.

Though the rest wasn't... well, you try to explain a family-
sized pack of Durex Magnums to an old lady in for passport
renewal.

ALICE. I mean, he just looks – harmless. He's always looked –

Beat.

Yeah. Everyone helped.

Most with smiles on their faces. Because he was so English
about it. 'I'm sorry. I'm sorry. I'm sorry. Did anyone get hit?
Did anyone get hit by my parmesan cheese? Has the
Marmite spilt?'

I mean – (*Laughs.*) the things he was packing.

He had a blow-up fuck sheep – (*Laughs.*) If that's not – if
that's not the greatest thing...

PHIL. At least the porn was hidden on the dongle. It'd have
been terrible if there'd been porn just lying across the – no.
No porn visible. The baa-baa fuck sheep on the other hand...

ALICE. And eventually everyone went on with their days and for some reason – for some reason – I – I was the last one helping.

And I'm not a nice person normally.

PHIL. Up to that point I'd had no idea she was deaf. So that was – that was – well, quite exotic frankly.

Pause. He smiles.

ALICE. The post office gave us another box – free of charge because they found it funny too – and we refilled it. (*Beat.*) And then we got the postage sorted. And I kept – helping.

PHIL. Thirty-four-pound postage. And he wasn't that grateful really.

ALICE. I don't know why I kept helping – I'm not nice – people don't – people don't think I'm nice.

PHIL. To be honest, I think he was quite surprised by some of the contents and not sure how to react. Not so much overwhelmed as – you know – scared. We're not very close really.

ALICE. And then he – he posted his large package – no metaphor – no – and I posted mine and – then he said –

PHIL. Thanks.

ALICE. And I said 'okay', and then he asked me for coffee.

PHIL. I had an – I'm not normally that confident. I don't make assumptions. It was a shot in the dark – I think it was the way she looked at me – or maybe it was the fact she was – I do like exotic.

ALICE. And I'd just come out of quite a difficult relationship. And he looked – harmless…

PHIL. And I mean, a coffee's a coffee. But, still…

ALICE. And so I said – yes…

PHIL. And we talked and she turned out to be a really good lip-reader.

ALICE. I think he liked the deaf thing a bit too much – but otherwise – he turned out to be – nice – nice and harmless.

PHIL. And she was – she is, gorgeous… which makes the, I mean, the confidence to ask out a gorgeous… Maybe only gorgeous to me.

Objectively probably a seven.

And a coffee's only a coffee. But…

Pause.

ALICE. I grab his dick.

PHIL. She's never been subtle in bed. Good-looking women rarely are.

ALICE. I don't build up to it, I just grab it – he's – quite – hard…

PHIL. A semi-on has never been hard for me.

I like that word semi-on.

I can stay at semi-on for days. I frequently do. Hard is harder, but semi-on…

ALICE. And I start masturbating it.

PHIL. In her fist. In her fist. I've often tried to change the position of her… It's the good-looking thing, you see… She's objectively a seven and sevens – they just – don't…

ALICE. Up and down, I feel it get harder.

PHIL. She's like a baby holding a rattle. Tring-tring. I feel like stopping her. I don't stop her.

ALICE. I feel it get harder. His dick is –

PHIL. Tring-tring. Tring-tring. She doesn't even retain good rhythm. I think it's because rhythm is far less important to girls than boys. Clitorally I mean.

ALICE. I feel it get – harder.

PHIL. Consider this: tring. Though girls are generally better dancers, day to day the best dancers – and by best, I mean, the best – tend to be male.

Michael Jackson. Prince.

ALICE. And then I start to prepare to go down on him.

PHIL. That Russian guy. Rudolph Nureythingy. Timberlake. Michael Flatley.

I think we're probably better dancers, men, we just – lack the confidence and the practice. Tring. Because I think rhythm is more important to us. Sexually. Tring. Tring.

ALICE. Kissing, licking his neck…

PHIL. She licks my neck. Tring. She kisses it. Tring.

ALICE. Licking it.

PHIL. She's a good neck kisser. I always like people kissing my neck.

Vampire thing I suppose… Tring tring tring.

ALICE. He tastes of vaguely of lemon zest and vinegar. I move down slowly. Kissing his nipple.

PHIL *laughs*.

What?

Beat.

PHIL. It tickles. Sorry.

ALICE. It – tickles?

PHIL. It's always tickled.

ALICE. It –

PHIL. Sorry. Carry on –

ALICE. I didn't mean to tickle you.

PHIL. Carry on –

ALICE. Is this okay?

PHIL. Yeah. It's nice.

ALICE. Are you…?

PHIL. It's nice.

There's a beat.

ALICE. Kissing his ribs.

PHIL. She kisses my ribs.

ALICE. He's gotten thinner. Didn't have much to lose, but lost it. He's not ate much since the… not eaten… not – he's not starving himself… Just – not breakfast or lunch. Only dinner.

Dinner we eat together. He's not much of an attention-seeker really. He doesn't want me to notice you see… He doesn't like to – he's kinder than that. We eat dinner together, mostly takeaways, so he eats that. Because I'd notice – that. I eat breakfast and lunch too, they aren't takeaways. But he doesn't. Eat them. He hasn't. He isn't. He's always been thin. He's getting thinner.

And then I'm kissing and licking his belly button.

PHIL. There was a girl in school became known as belly job, because she thought licking out a belly button was the same as giving a blow job.

ALICE. And then I'm taking the head of his dick in my mouth… I start gently massaging around the outside of it with my tongue. His bell end is sticky. There's white-yellow substance under the rim.

PHIL. And I just try and concentrate. For some reason blow jobs are always the occasion when I lose my – I don't know why…

ALICE. I lick it up. I swallow it. It tastes horrible. A mixture of chicken fat, yogurt past its sell-by and the smell in the kitchen when you leave your washing up in the sink for five days.

I start moving up and down –

PHIL. I wouldn't mind it if she didn't do it really. Go. Down. I'm not licking her out. I'm just not…

ALICE. I remove my mouth and gently blow on the outside of his long hard –

PHIL. I'm not sucking her tit either – I tried before – I got a mouthful of breast milk – when we last tried to have sex. Two weeks ago.

I haven't been able to get the taste out since.

This sort of sugary watery milk. The erection is wilting. Maybe I'm concentrating too hard.

ALICE. And then I swallow the bulb of his dick again and I'm moving faster now. Faster and harder. Going lower and lower. Almost gagging as I try and push it down the back of my mouth…

PHIL. She always tries to deep-throat. She can't. The erection is wilting. I can feel it start to topple.

ALICE. Trying everything to make him – almost gagging…

PHIL (*vocalisation of despair*).

ALICE. Phil?

PHIL. I know.

ALICE. Am I…?

PHIL. No.

ALICE. Because you're –

PHIL. I know. Sorry. It's got a –

Beat.

ALICE. Phil –

PHIL. I know.

ALICE. It's just –

PHIL. Yeah, it's not –

ALICE. Hard.

Beat.

PHIL. I think I've got a bit of a tummy…

ALICE. Oh.

Pause.

PHIL. Yeah. I'm not feeling well. Tummy. Or… Just temporary not feeling well. I'll be back in a minute. Think of it like a lunch break.

ALICE. Right.

Pause.

PHIL. I worked out the best route.

A twenty-minute drive.

Well… Twenty-four on a bad day. Seventeen on a good. The best route that is. Of course it could have started when I was at work and she'd have had to take a taxi and I – I'd have tried to give the taxi driver directions then.

I should have written it down – the directions – to give the taxi driver. In case that… I didn't. It didn't.

Me and my maps.

ALICE. He did about fifteen trial runs. All in all.

I think. In the end.

Google Maps gave him three different routes. He tried them all. Five times. Just in case.

PHIL. I have always been a fan of practice.

Not in a sort of practice-makes-perfect sort of way. Because I've never believed in perfect.

ALICE. He was – scientific – he was very scientific about it.

He's a very scientific guy.

PHIL. It's just too much of an abstract construct for me. Perfect.

ALICE. Which is not to mean… He's not a scientist.

He got a B in Combined Science at GCSE and then gave it up. But then he didn't do that well at any of his GCSEs. I was better at my GCSEs than he was at his.

PHIL. I believe you can get better at something.

ALICE. How well do you have to know someone to know they got a B in Science GCSE?

PHIL. I believe you can be good at something. But I'd never trust someone who told me they were perfect at something.

In fact, I've never seen, heard, or smelt perfect. Perfection.

ALICE. I won't list all his GCSEs – but I know them… Most of them. He did best in history.

I suppose it's sweet – knowing what he got – but –

PHIL. Perfect song? No. It'd have to be one that I'd want to hear whatever mood I was in, whatever time of day it was. Doesn't exist.

Perfect film? Definitely no. And I probably know more about films than I do music.

Perfect food? Not even chicken.

Now I was at school with someone who did a perfect Michael Jackson Moonwalk impression. I was nine. He was nine. It probably wasn't perfect.

ALICE. I went on seven – trial runs – with him. But then I stopped – he was – he was trying so hard he was sweating. Every time.

I was eight months. I didn't sweat.

PHIL. It was seventeen minutes on optimal distance… And that includes – from the picking-up of the case to the arrival in maternity reception.

Interesting, the route I ended up picking wasn't the recommended Google Maps route, but their secondary option.

ALICE. And actually the seventh trial run was perfect, so I've
no idea what he did after that.

PHIL. But I think they liked me.

Most people like me.

ALICE. Perfect. He hates the use of the word perfect. But if
something can't get any better – it's perfect, right? You see, I
have no problem with relative concepts.

He does.

PHIL. That's not an arrogant... Only because I'm – harmless.

That's anti-arrogant.

ALICE. I actually – this is probably wrong – I actually got to
thinking he was using it as an excuse to get away from me.
'Just out for another trial run, darling.' Not that he – we
don't use words like darling. 'Just out for another trial run
so...' But actually he'd just park up somewhere.

It's probably wrong. Just one of those thoughts you can't get
out of your head.

No, no, the truth is, he didn't have much of a reason to get
away from me then.

Beat.

PHIL. And then she started. She, uh –

ALICE. There was this – blood –

PHIL. She bled.

ALICE. Just this – blood –

PHIL. This –

ALICE. I thought it was discharge of some – I rationalised – I –
put a tampon up there.

PHIL. She woke me up. We talked about it and she put a
tampon up there.

We thought it was – spotting.

ALICE. I didn't want to stain the sheets.

PHIL. We didn't want to stain the sheets.

  Blood is very hard to get out.

  It was 3 a.m.

ALICE. Just a – tampon.

PHIL. She woke me again half-hour later –

ALICE. Phil –

PHIL. And her hand – her hand was covered in this – blood…

ALICE. Phil – Phil – Phil –

PHIL. Yeah.

ALICE. Phil – Phil – Phil –

PHIL. Yeah? Yeah. What?

ALICE. Phil Phil Phil.

PHIL. Her hand was – the tampon wasn't –

ALICE. My – hand was –

PHIL. Actually never saw the tampon again. Must of a… The – sort of metallic. It smelt sort of metallic.

ALICE. My hand –

PHIL. But not metallic like period blood. It smelt like different blood to period blood. I know the smell of period blood. It wasn't – that.

ALICE. My hand was – Phil – Phil –

PHIL. She – it took nineteen minutes, my eyes were blurry. It was four in the morning it should have taken seventeen minutes.

  There wasn't too much traffic at four in the morning… so that's practice – that's practice –

ALICE. I was sitting and bleeding and sitting and bleeding –

PHIL. There's still a bloodstain on the passenger seat of my car today actually. I tried to get it out but… I tried everything to get it out… I tell people it was the dog.

I've told one person. The dog. I tell – people.

Blood is very hard to get out.

Beat.

ALICE. I'm rushed in –

PHIL. The reception takes one look at us and knows we're not going to stop.

ALICE. He is shouting – 'now' – for some reason – he shouts 'now' for some reason.

PHIL. NOW. NOW. I was worried because some of the doctors have not always understood her.

ALICE. Not 'help' – just now –

PHIL. NOW. NOW.

ALICE. Nurses rush out to… doctors and… he keeps shouting…

PHIL. NOW. NOW. And they've got her fingers up her and in her – up her – in her – and they're all frowning at each other and…

ALICE. They start feeling my belly. Feeling inside me. Hands everywhere.

PHIL. Hands everywhere.

They don't stop. They don't ask. We don't want them to.

ALICE. Hands. Where's the blood coming from? It's like a musical number without the music. Hands.

PHIL. Maybe you'd like to step outside. This nurse says.

ALICE. And I look up and for him.

PHIL. I'm not stepping outside. I'm not – stepping. The nurse tries to shepherd, but I sheep back. She's not making any noise at all.

That's the funny thing she's not screaming –

ALICE. And it's like I can see everything – everywhere –

PHIL. She's not making a noise – not a sound –

ALICE. These hands – I'm like a – like a musical – I feel like a hand – I can't lip-read enough to work out what's going on and Phil is just standing there – helpless –

PHIL. And then they stop. They shouldn't be stopping.

ALICE. They – stop.

PHIL. They look at each other – they've all got such big eyebrows.

ALICE. They step back like one – like a musical –

PHIL. They nod at each other and step back –

ALICE. And then I feel like screaming.

PHIL. In actual fact if I'd have timed it from the moment of NOW. NOW. Getting in the – NOW. NOW. To the – to the – stepping back – to the doctor telling – telling – us – probably not five minutes – probably not – so it's not difficult to… It's not a complicated diagnosis.

Five minutes and he just knows… Five minutes from when he saw us to knowing. That is not a long…

That's not long.

He peels off his latex gloves. He peels them off. Very bloody. Maybe he took the tampon out surreptitiously when no one was. Maybe she… We never saw the tampon again. And his hands – droop. Very droopy hands. Which is surprising because they were – very useful – hands.

And he turns and he looks at me, and he looks at me. And then at her.

And… uh… The other doctor doesn't leave. Nurses. Two nurses. They don't. They've stopped. More or less. But… uh… they don't.

Leave.

That's – I suppose he can't take us outside – she's sort of strapped in. But if I was him I'd have asked the others to leave. Instead, he just takes off these bloodstained gloves revealing his droopy hands and he checks his sleeves for more blood – and he says – we think it's a – he doesn't say 'I'm really sorry, it's a – '

He says – we think it's an – he doesn't say sorry – but maybe that's his technique. I don't think I'd want him to apologise. Or express sympathy.

He just says plain – plainly – plain –

Droopy hands. Leaning over Alice so she can lip-read him.

'We think it's an antepartum haemorrhage…'

ALICE. Antepartum…

PHIL. Antepartum

Pause.

Antepartum.

ALICE. Antepartum.

PHIL. Said backwards – mutrap – etan. No. Mutrap etna.

No.

Yes.

Mutrap etna.

Pause.

Said backwards…

ALICE. Antepartum.

Pause.

PHIL. When she first got pregnant my dad asked me – pretty regularly actually – whether I thought I was ready.

Beat.

ALICE. Antepartum –

PHIL. He asked me in a way that made perfectly clear he was pretty sure I wasn't.

It's all about emphasis. Are you ready? Are you really ready?

I don't know which word you need to emphasise to say it like him. But it is. All about emphasis. Or your eyes when you say it.

He's got big eyebrows too.

Pause.

I thought I was. I was.

Ready.

We'd actually been trying for one.

And if you try… well, then you are ready.

What I mean is…

It wasn't a mistake. And when we thought she WAS ready Alice let me wait in the loo with her while she pissed on the stick, and we're really not –

Really not –

Not the sort of couple that does the whole sharing-toilet thing together.

It wasn't a mistake –

Pause.

ALICE. The placenta had separated too early so that – sounds like a knock-knock joke that… Knock-knock. Who's – uh –

PHIL. Antepartum.

Mutrap – etna.

And I… And you know when your face is dropping –
drooping – like his hands –

And the doctor says – this doctor – the baby's going to – the
baby is – the blood supply to the baby has been – cut off
so… The baby is… the baby was…

Pause.

ALICE. On our second date, he took me to see *Spartacus*.

PHIL. It was showing at the NFT. It's a classic.

ALICE. I'd never seen it.

PHIL. It's – I mean, classic is overused as a word. Sometimes
classic just means old. But for me – classic… There's this bit
– I won't spoil it for anyone – but, you know, I am
Spartacus.

ALICE. It was quite a long film for a second date. I mean, when
a film is over three hours long – it's close to three-and-half
hours. And it wasn't subtitled.

PHIL. I didn't want to – I thought – she said she didn't worry
about that kind of thing –

No. I am Spartacus. No. I am Spartacus. And Kirk Douglas.
Standing with tears rolling down his face. I am Spartacus.

The chance to see a classic inside a cinema. You don't get
that very often. And this was it at its best. The one-hundred-
and-ninety-eight-minute re-restored re-release.

ALICE. And an average date is – what? Four hours long. Four
hours minus almost three and half hours – you're not going
to have much face time. You need to – most people talk on
dates. But he took me to see *Spartacus*.

PHIL. I mean, probably a bad idea, show her a film full of big
men in the little pants. When I am a little man in big pants.
But I think she liked it.

Beat.

ALICE. I liked it. He took my hand about halfway through.

PHIL. I took her hand to squeeze it, about halfway through, instinctive thing, because it was one of my favourite bits, the bit with – I don't want to spoil it, but Olivier is being a fucking don – and I wanted to communicate 'this is one of my favourite bits' – and I don't like talking in the cinema and so I thought – time for a bit of non-verbal communication...

After I squeezed it, I just sort of – held on. Hung on.

ALICE. And he made me feel like –

PHIL. And I don't know.

Holding hands with a gorgeous girl in a cinema while watching your favourite film.

There aren't many better moments.

I mean, frame that moment. Put it on your hallway wall. Beside your poster of *Octopussy*.

Pause.

ALICE. The third date he said I could choose.

PHIL. We went to the Tate for our third date. Her idea. I suggested she choose where we went because it always feels weird deciding everything, and I know men are supposed to be the runners and the riders in these situations, but...

ALICE. It was sweet. It was very him. Him saying, I want to take you on a third date, but I'd like you to choose where we go.

PHIL. I know nothing about art. I mean – nothing. To me, an exhibition of film posters – that I'd like – but art... I mean, in some ways, going to an art gallery, my kind of hell, because – I spend the entire time thinking – how long do I stare at this thing? How much time do I spend looking at the notes – frankly the only interesting bit – I like a biography...

ALICE. I was on an improve-myself thing. I was on a impress-him-with-my-sophisticated-choices.

PHIL. And what do you say? I mean, do you just say – I like this one... or do you say – I love what the painter's done with perspective and softness of colour?

ALICE. I do like art. But I don't really go to galleries.

PHIL. Or do you say – oh in these notes, it says he fucked his sister and killed his mum. Interesting. I can see why he used so much pink...

ALICE. I just – he felt the kind of guy I could stretch myself with... And I did want to impress him.

PHIL. Still – this time she took my hand as we looked around this exhibit by some such about some such. I was probably a bit clammy. My hand was, because I was nervous to say the right things about perspective and softness of pink. But it was nice. Her touching me.

ALICE. It was on the fourth date – the fourth date – he kissed me.

PHIL. We'd just had a nice dinner. Fourth date.

Nice dinner. Lots of talking.

She talked about her previous relationships, I tried not to talk about my lack of previous relationships. Bit of wine. Bit of food.

Free after-dinner mints afterwards.

Walk down to the Thames. My idea. Would you like to see the river? I like a river after a meal.

I'd learnt some sign.

ALICE. He'd learnt some sign.

PHIL. I signed [I like you]. (*Long bad finger-spelling.*)

ALICE. To this day I still have no idea what he signed – but it was sweet he tried.

PHIL. I signed [I like you]. (*Again long bad finger-spelling.*)

ALICE. It was sweet.

PHIL. I signed –

Attempts to sign again, ALICE *stops him.*

'I like you' on a bridge. And then I kissed her.

ALICE. He kissed me on a bridge.

That's kind of classy.

It wasn't sunset. If it'd been sunset. Even better. It was night. But still, kissing on a bridge, full marks. He did well. I was pleased to be kissed. But also – this sounds entirely stupid – pleased for him. That's meant less arrogant than it sounds. I just meant – he did it right.

And that's the thing about Phil – you want him to do well – you want him to transcend.

PHIL. I don't make moves on many women.

But kissing Alice… on a bridge. Our mouths sort of fitted. And I always knew they would.

They kiss.

The baby is –

ALICE. The baby – was –

PHIL. The baby – is – was –

ALICE. The – baby –

PHIL. Baby –

ALICE. The first sex…

Well, it was… energetic.

I invited him back to mine. Fifth date. I said, come to mine, I'll cook you dinner.

Have you knocked yet?

PHIL. Yeah I just did it.

But then there was the whole sex mountain to climb. Bing-bing-bing. Sex mountain. Like a ride at a theme park. But far more… I'd really like to go on a ride at a theme park called Sex Mountain.

It had been a while. I was really nervous. I mean, it's really not like riding a bike. Sex. It's far more complicated. Gears. Levers. Knobs. Twiddly bits. Wet bits. Dry bits. Rough bits. Smooth bits. Tring tring.

ALICE. I'd let him choose the tunes while I got the wine from the fridge.

ALICE *exits*.

PHIL. She had a terrible range of music.

Then I found the Straits and all was well…

Music: Dire Straits 'Romeo and Juliet' plays. PHIL sings along to the second verse.

As ALICE *re-enters*, PHIL *looks up and begins to improvise sign to express the lyrics to her. This sounds as bad as it is but he is very enthusiastic about it. She watches, amused. She works out the song with a grin.*

ALICE. Dire Straits: 'Romeo and Juliet'.

PHIL *takes her in his arms, they dance awkwardly, and then they dance less awkwardly. They kiss.*

He was – he is a good kisser. Receptive.

They kiss.

PHIL. I mean, as long as you concentrate on the lyrics you're more or less fine…

They kiss.

ALICE. I wasn't expecting to fuck him. It just sort of happened – I mean, he's basically Tigger and…

PHIL. I was so busy concentrating on the lyrics…

ALICE. I tell you, once you've been to bed with Tigger. You don't look back.

PHIL. Mark Knopfler, I have a lot to thank you for. Happy amateurs. I salute you.

ALICE. And if you've never had anyone fuck you whilst singing along with Dire Straits. I'd thoroughly recommend it.

It was loving. It was touching. It was genuinely enthusiastic.

Pause.

PHIL. The baby is –

ALICE. The baby – was –

PHIL. The baby – is – was –

ALICE. Shall I get a cup of tea?

PHIL. We lie still. I can sense her disappointment.

ALICE. My breath tastes of dick. Or something like dick. Or whatever it tasted like before plus dick.

PHIL. I can sense her disappointment.

ALICE. Shall I get you a cup of tea?

PHIL. No. Let's just lie here for a bit.

ALICE. If it's stomach you probably need something to settle it.

PHIL. I know. But let's just lie here for a bit.

ALICE. Sometimes – I look at you – and –

PHIL. Yeah?

ALICE. Doesn't matter.

PHIL. No. Okay.

ALICE. Shall I get you a cup of tea, Phil?

PHIL. Yeah. Okay.

And she walks out of bed. Her arse still…

ALICE. Be back in five.

PHIL. And I'm alone in our bedroom again.

I touch my dick.

I masturbate it slightly. More – just to check it's okay.

There is nothing worse than – not getting the reassurance
you need after a moment of crisis. And my dick was deflated
and that helps no one.

So bit of casual balloon work – bit of masturbation – what's
it going to be, kids? A balloon dog? A snake. A giraffe? I
hear her on the stairs.

I stop masturbating. If there's one thing she doesn't need to
see it's…

But it won't go down it won't go…

ALICE (*calling*). Tea's made.

Tea's made.

She hands him the mug.

PHIL. Thanks. She doesn't look at my erection.

She lies down in bed beside me.

ALICE. I lie down – in bed beside my – husband – with his
average-sized erect penis.

PHIL. I take a sup of the tea. It still has the bag in. She's left the
bag in too long. It's too strong. And slowly my erection goes
down. Its timing is really off today.

ALICE. And I try and keep as still as possible.

Pause.

PHIL. The baby is –

ALICE. The baby – was –

PHIL. The baby – is – was –

ALICE. The – baby –

PHIL. Antepartum –

ALICE. Antepartum –

PHIL. Mutrap-etna. Sounds like an Indian cure for bowel cancer.

ALICE. Antepartum.

PHIL. She looks at me –

She looks at me – like it's my fault.

Not – she's got a thing she does with her eyes – not...

Your average layperson – wouldn't be able to read it – but I'm not your average layperson, I am an expert, where she is concerned, and I do...

I know her.

I an expert on her – it's all in the eyes.

Though – actually – it is only a think in this case – I think – I think she's looking at me like it's my fault. It could just be – she could just be –

Because the thing is, I can't see her – face, because I'm not looking. I think she's looking at me like it's my fault. She's just staring at me. I can feel it. But – I can't look at her.

ALICE. And he can't look at me.

And I can see him breathe.

I can see the noise inside his nostrils.

I can feel his oxygen.

I can feel all of him.

There is a dead baby inside me.

Floating like a sack of blood.

Inside me –

And I can't feel that at all.

Pause.

PHIL. And I still can't look at her.

ALICE. And I want to tear myself open and cut the spider out.

Beat.

PHIL. Six months later I'd moved in.

ALICE. Before I know it he'd moved in...

PHIL. Her place was better than mine, we thought we might as well share rents, as we were spending basically every night together already.

ALICE. He was spending every night at mine – his wasn't very central – and so we sort of – well, I mean, it was as pragmatic as deciding to split the rent. We've never had much money.

PHIL. Six months. Quite quick. First time I'd lived with a woman.

ALICE. So – he moved in. His suggestion. But I didn't – object. And the first thing he did was arrange our cups in height order. Then he did my pictures, adding his pictures, and making them in height order. In fact, he more or less arranged everything in height order. He has slight OCD. I liked it.

PHIL. A woman woman you understand? I mean, I'd lived with women before – at college I lived with three – but this was...

ALICE. He made my life fun. He – because he's such a div – he –

PHIL. And then – it was like everything was pre-programmed, mortgage – well, renting you feel like you're throwing your money away...

ALICE. And he'd always find new ways of doing things – because he had to get up for work earlier than me – for instance – this was after he'd shared my bed and left my bed before me for about six months – but he started leaving me Post-its on the pillow – and then a flower – and then a variety of strange things – and then he started to try and surprise me.

PHIL. And then we were in a… momentum… I suppose. I
learnt a bit of sign – not much – she lip-read so well. And
I've never been good at languages. But she didn't mind.

ALICE. He tried to learn sign – but he was shit. So I told him to
give up.

PHIL. I liked her friends. She thought my friends were strange.
We just kind of slotted together.

ALICE. For our anniversary – of us meeting in the post office –
I forgot it, he didn't – he left this – like – this baby lamb
beside the bed. Actual real-life lamb – and I woke up with it
staring at me – him laughing by the door – I almost shit
myself – it was – amazing – and then we had to get rid of it
because the neighbours complained about the noise and he
said we could find it a new home or we could eat it. He
thought there was something spiritual about eating it. So we
did. And then both threw up because we couldn't cope with
the idea. But even that was funny.

PHIL. Pretty quickly, I knew I wanted to marry her. So I just
sort of… asked. Well, I say that like it was an accident. It
wasn't an accident.

ALICE. You don't want to know how he asked me to marry him.

PHIL. I'm not going to go in to how I asked her to marry me. It
didn't go well. Needless to say I aimed for another joke
thing…

ALICE. Even the wedding day was fun – funny. I mean
sometimes he made a complete balls-up of things. And he's
never as funny in the way he intends. But he tries – he tried
so hard – and –

PHIL. But she still said yes.

ALICE. He tried so hard. And he loves – loved me – so much.

PHIL. And we got married at this simple church in Tottenham
Hale and when she said 'I will'. Did you know it was 'I will'
not 'I do'? When she said 'I will'. Aaron Lennon scored an
eighty-ninth-minute winner and the cheers from White Hart
Lane transcended the room.

True story. I got my mate to record *Match of the Day* that night. I still have it.

ALICE. He couldn't take his eyes off me the whole of the wedding day. But he also couldn't keep his eyes off me the rest of the time. He couldn't stop looking at me.

PHIL. And then – marital bliss – marital bliss –

ALICE. And I couldn't take my eyes off him. Looking at me.

PHIL. This wonderful woman. This wonderful thing. This – I mean, genuinely, she – marital bliss.

ALICE. And he's there…

Trying to make it nice for everyone – but me.

PHIL. The people – the person – I am looking at is… The doctor. Because it must be terrible this bit. I mean, I'm a big fan of empathy, and I – I wouldn't do his job so… you know, it must be terrible this bit. So I'm trying not to make it too hard for him.

ALICE. And the doctor says – leaning over me – so I can't just read his lips, I can watch his tongue – a large pink thing covered in mucus – the thing is –

You're going to have to go through labour.

PHIL. I'm not listening to what he's saying. I've got this sort of ringing in my ears – like when I've been to a gig – not that I – I don't go to many gigs. I'm trying to just smile at him. To not make it too hard – for him.

ALICE. You're going to have to go through labour.

PHIL. What?

ALICE. What?

PHIL. He says – I pick it up on my outside antennae – you're going to have to go through labour.

ALICE. You're going to have to go through labour.

PHIL. The baby is – . I mean, I've understood that much.

ALICE. The baby is dead. But you're going to have to go through labour anyway.

PHIL. The baby is dead. But you're going to have to go through labour anyway. A Caesarean section is possible – but he'd really rather not because it could damage – damage –

ALICE. Our future chances of having a baby.

PHIL. And now I look at her.

Pause.

The baby is – dead. But conventional birthing would be the best thing for making sure your birth organs – whatever you call them – are intact – were we to – later – want another try at having a baby which isn't – dead. Now I can look at her.

And she can't look at me.

And I'm really looking at her now – I'm super looking at her now – I'm looking at her like there's no one else on earth. Now. Which there sort of isn't.

But she doesn't look like she's going to cry. And she doesn't want to share it with me. This – whatever this is.

ALICE. And then I turn and I sit up and I straddle him. I straddle him on his stomach.

And I lean down and I kiss his neck.

His neck and then his ear and then his neck again.

I look at him.

PHIL. Third wedding anniversary – I said let's try for a baby. I just – said – let's try for a baby. You see, I know for a fact my mum had to persuade my dad to have me and my brother. So I thought –

ALICE. And he's got this look on his face.

PHIL. She was – I mean, I'd read it's good to try before she's thirty. To optimise. It's something very specific to our age, how late people try for babies. And I thought – I thought I wanted her to have my baby.

Let's have a baby.

We were watching the news.

ALICE. I'm on top of him.

PHIL. Probably it was about starving kids or Aids orphans or… something that makes you feel maternal you know… paternal…

ALICE. If I'm touching myself then so can he.

PHIL. And before I know it, I'm sitting on the bath watching her piss on a stick.

ALICE. It's sort of a deal we've got.

PHIL. Best. Thing. Ever.

ALICE. And we're making pure –

PHIL. Well, that and holding hands at *Spartacus* and Aaran Lennon's winner.

ALICE. Eye contact.

PHIL. Best thing. Girls don't make the same piss sounds we do. More of a gush. Best. Thing. Ever.

ALICE. And he –

PHIL. And I –

ALICE. And he's hard again.

They both smile.

And then I lean up, and I look at him and he knows and he positions himself – he holds his dick in his hand and just sort of points it up – we're used to this –

PHIL. She does this face that's a half-moan. I do find it sexy.

ALICE. We're used to this.

PHIL. I'm hard again.

ALICE. And then I take him – take him – inside me.

Pause.

PHIL. And – that moment when you're inside a woman is just – breathe in.

Breathe out.

ALICE. And – I feel him inside me like an alien – like something – breathe in.

Breathe out.

PHIL. And – she's warm, I feel warm – breathe in.

Breathe out.

ALICE. And I start gently moving up and down on him. On the alien.

Breathe in.

Breathe out.

PHIL. And I slip my hand between her buttocks and start massaging her anus again.

Breathe in.

ALICE. And I hold every now and again so I can feel the whole of him inside me. But then I go back to my gentle rhythm.

Breathe out.

PHIL. My finger slips inside and as she moves up and down so I keep my finger inside – breathe in.

ALICE. Labour is induced by means of a membrane sweep – he explains with Marmite breath – the doctor – he says what I'm going to do is sever the membranes holding the baby into me. Onto me.

Breathe out.

PHIL. And then I move my other hand up so it's holding her hair. Breathe in.

ALICE. The contractions start quickly. The baby has nothing to hold itself to me. My body starts to force it out. The baby starts to force itself out. Ahhh. Breathe out.

PHIL. And she holds me inside her and squeezes herself together as hard as she can and she sort of smiles at me – her eyes glazed – breathe in.

ALICE. Ahhh. It's there. Breathe out.

PHIL. We fall over onto our side, and then over and round and I'm on top and my finger is still in her arsehole so I have to pull it hard – breathe in.

ALICE. Yes, it's coming. It's – Ah-ahh – breathe out.

PHIL. I lie down close over the top of her and start moving faster and she looks scared like I might try and kiss her – she doesn't like me kissing her – breathe in.

ALICE *is going into labour now.*

ALICE. AHHHH. And everyone's fucking smiling at me.

PHIL. She stops me, she pushes herself off me – she turns over onto her back, she kneels up, she wants me to fuck her from behind – I oblige. She likes this – it means I can go deeper inside her.

ALICE. AHHHH. I want to be numb. I want to be numb.

PHIL. And I grab her hair, harder now, she likes me to grab her hair harder and I pull it round my fist, her filthy unwashed hair and I pull her up, so that as I fuck her I can see her face –

ALICE. AHHHHHH. They look at me pleased. If someone else tells me I'm doing well, I'm going to rip their head off and shit in their throat.

PHIL. She grabs my nipple… And twists it hard. Ah.

ALICE. AHHHHHHHHH. And then I feel it start to shift. I feel it start to shift. I can feel it move. I can feel it come down. I didn't think I'd be able to feel it shift.

PHIL. And I'm sweating. I feel the sweat beading up on me. Her sweat. My sweat. Our sweet sweat.

ALICE. AHHHHHHHHH. And he's just standing there and he's just standing there. And I feel it come down I feel it shift. I feel like a shit unused pinball machine!

PHIL. And she's – ahhh – grabbing my balls as she – she's just squeezing me like –

ALICE. AHHHHHHHHHHH. The doctor puts his hand up me and then smiles. I don't care if it damages future prospects. I just can't do it. I want it cut out, I say. I want it gone. And the doctor just smiles and pats me as if I – haven't – spoken.

PHIL. I start to build up to a hard pace now. In withdraw. In withdraw. In withdraw. In withdraw.

ALICE. AHHHHHHHHHHHHHHHHH. And he tells me it's coming and Phil grips my hand tight and then he looks in the other direction. He fucking looks in the other direction. I don't care if he's crying. I've got a thing shifting inside me. I want it gone.

AHHHHHHHH. I FEEL IT SHIFT. THIS HURTS. CUT IT OUT.

PHIL. And I think she's getting wetter. She's either getting wetter or bleeding…

ALICE. AHHHHHHHHHH. And he tells me he can see the head. The doctor. CUT IT OUT. PLEASE. CUT IT OUT. I HURT. I FUCKING HURT.

PHIL. And I'm sort of – I feel powerful –

ALICE. AAAAH. OW. OW. OW.

PHIL. I feel so fucking powerful.

ALICE. The doctor's got his forceps. And he's pulling to get its shoulders through. FUCK. FUCK. FUCKING Ah-Ah-AAAAAAAh

PHIL. I feel amazing…

ALICE. I'M HURT. I'M HURT. I'M HURT. AHHHHH.

PHIL. I like the way you can feel it when you're about to come.
I like the feeling of it surging up inside you, like fuel on a
computer game...

ALICE. I CAN'T DO THIS. I CAN'T DO THIS.

PHIL. And then I'm – ah –

ALICE screams.

Ah –

*ALICE screams. A chilling powerful scream. The scream of
a woman giving birth to a dead baby.*

Rope after rope of cum. I really needed this –

Pause.

ALICE. Ow... Ah... Ow...

*Pause. A long horrible pause. The couple breathe almost in
unison. Seriously out of breath. PHIL gets the chair and
brings it downstage and sits her down.*

PHIL. I'll get you some water.

Pause.

ALICE. They ask if I want to hold it.

They say it'll be better if I do.

They say they'll wrap it in a towel and give it to me and
hold. I feel like saying I'd rather have the chips unwrapped.
I'll eat them straight away.

I don't – I can't –

Pause.

They ask if I want to hold it. No. No. No. I can't hold it.

Pause.

They ask if I want to hold it. I think the nurse calls her 'it' by
accident.

Pause.

It was a girl.

Pause.

I don't hold her, and nor – does he.

They sit in silence for an age. Both still breathing quite heavily.

He took me to Brighton.

The day we got out of the hospital.

We got out. I got out.

Of the hospital.

I got out about 10 a.m. after doctor's first rounds, and he was waiting for me.

He drove me down to Brighton – didn't announce it, just did it – got me in the car and just – kept driving – and we went for a walk along the front. He then bought me this sausage-and-chips-in-a-bucket thing which was hideous but nicely – hideous.

I mean, yeah, it was nice.

He didn't eat.

I didn't notice that then.

And then we sat on the stones and we didn't speak to each other for ages and then he turned his head, turned to look at me and asked me if I wanted to go play the 2p machines on the pier.

I said no.

Beat.

He didn't – touch me – the entire time in Brighton.

Actually, the entire day.

I mean, not once, he didn't touch me – nudge me – he is a nudger – to say 'oh, look at those fat birds struggling in the wind, they've eaten one too many tourist chips' or 'doesn't the sea look beautiful with the sun setting on it like that'.

He didn't touch me to hold my hand.

He even avoided touching me when he was changing gears in the car.

My leg was right on the edge of the passenger seat, and not once, the entire journey, did he accidentally nudge me when changing from first to second. Which means, to avoid accidents you must really try.

He didn't say he was doing it – but that night post our Brighton stony-beach adventures – he didn't drive me home – he drove me to a hotel.

Near the house. He drove me almost home, but then we – swerved – and ended up at a – hotel.

We'd had dinner there once on Valentine's Day.

He drove me, and we went upstairs and they let us into the room and we both got undressed and got into bed and he let me put my arm on him.

I don't know whether it was deliberate not going home. That house. That bed.

I had loads of thoughts when I he, uh… Maybe he was trying to protect me from it. Maybe he thought he thought I wasn't ready to see it. Maybe he just couldn't cope with me inside our room. Not yet. So he thought he'd get used to me in another room. I don't know.

But it probably mostly was – as I found out – it probably mostly was – I found out – well, you see, he hadn't changed the sheets.

Beat.

He'd just – he'd slept around the blood. Not on it. Around it.

I think it was his way of… something.

I don't know.

– he probably just – realised if there was one thing I couldn't see that night it was dried-in blood on white sheets.

Blood that he'd slept around.

Anyway…

We burnt them.

In the end.

Like they were the sheets of a plague victim, or lice victim, or some – thing.

Pause.

PHIL. Okay?

ALICE. What?

PHIL. Okay?

ALICE. Yeah.

PHIL. Yeah?

ALICE. Yeah.

PHIL. Okay. I'm okay.

ALICE. Yeah? Yeah. Sorry, I should have – I should have asked.

Pause.

PHIL. I – I needed that –

ALICE. Did you?

PHIL. I think – we – needed that…

ALICE. Yeah.

Pause. The longest pause we can imagine.

PHIL. Did you…? Need that?

ALICE. Yeah.

PHIL. Yeah?

Beat.

ALICE. Yeah.

Pause. He signs as he speaks.

PHIL. I do – love you – you know that, right?

Beat.

ALICE. Yeah.

Beat.

PHIL. Yeah?

Beat.

ALICE. Yeah. And, uh, I l-o-v-e love you too.

PHIL. Good.

ALICE. Yeah?

Beat.

PHIL. Yeah.

A Nick Hern Book

The Solid Life of Sugar Water first published as a paperback original in Great Britain in 2015 by Nick Hern Books Limited, The Glasshouse, 49a Goldhawk Road, London W12 8QP, in association with Graeae Theatre Company and Theatre Royal Plymouth

The Solid Life of Sugar Water copyright © 2015 Jack Thorne

Jack Thorne has asserted his right to be identified as the author of this work

Cover image: ©iStock.com/pascalgenest; title treatment by Dragonfly Design

Designed and typeset by Nick Hern Books, London
Printed in Great Britain by CPI Group (UK) Ltd

A CIP catalogue record for this book is available from the British Library

ISBN   978 1 84842 513 2